The Social Media Compendium. Social Media Training for Businesses.

© Copyright 2016 by Michael Ingram

Website: - www.bonusincomegenerator.com

Twitter: - @seodummy1

Tsū: https://www.tsu.co/Bonusincome

This e book is licensed for your personal enjoyment only. It may not be re-sold or, given away to other people. If you would like to share this book with another Person, please purchase an additional copy for each recipient. If you're reading this and did not purchase it, or it was not purchased for your use only, please purchase your own copy from Amazon.com. Thank you for respecting the hard work of this Author.

Before we start delving into the World of Social Media and lots of secret tricks, hacks and hints to get you ahead of the 'pack', I would like to genuinely thank you from the bottom of my heart for choosing my book. There are other books on similar subjects out there and I'm really grateful you've chosen this book above the others. My aim is a simple one and that's to give you great content and value for money.

When you've taken all you want from this book (statistically most people never read a book from cover to cover) It would be really helpful to me if you could leave a few positive words in a review on Amazon. I'm like most people and appreciate approval and encouragement to keep me following my dreams to be productive as an Author.

Also, your positive feedback will help ensure others buy my books and hopefully help me earn a living (it's not as easy as it looks to produce a book)

Here is the link to review my book:....
http://amzn.to/2bVdIPA

I thank you once again for your custom and generosity. If you want more information on me or the other books, or, courses I have published, please visit my website :-

www.bonusincomegenerator.com

If you sign up on my site you will receive exclusive, extra content for free.

About the Author

Hi my name is Mike but my followers on Social Media call me SEODummy (amongst other things which I can't put in a book). As you can tell by the name I've given myself, I love all things related to SEO and social media but will always be learning more everyday hence the Dummy bit

There are plenty of so-called social media gurus out there who proclaim to know everything and anything about social media. I am not one of those so-called gurus and don't pretend to know everything about the world of social media.

However I have sent over 5000 tweets on the subject and managed to build large numbers of followers on many different formats of social media networks and would like to be able to share with you my knowledge of how to grow large numbers of quality, targeted followers. I also hope I can tell you of some of the things I have learnt about Search Engine optimisation and Social Media in order that you may grow your business in terms of both increasing your engaged customer levels and also increasing your profitability.

This book is dedicated to all of those who have shaped me to be the person I am including Mum, Dad and Karen and all of the many lovely people who have passed away, as well as the many others (happily living) who have put up with my insistence on being left in silence whilst writing this Book, including my lovely Family.

Table Of Contents

Table Of Contents 8

Introduction 10

What is Social Media? 12

10 reasons your business should be leveraging Social Media. 16

Main social media sites and which ones are the correct fit for your business? 22

What Is the Importance of Conducting a Social Media Audit? 22

Write quality content to expand your social networks 31

Understanding types of content 35

Creating content quickly 59

Content and SEO 63

Nine tips for increasing your click through rates on your Facebook Ads 65

The Ninja way of attracting customers on Facebook 71

The Five whys and how they're Important for your Social Media strategy 73

Reach your target audience on Twitter. 79

Growing circles on Google+ 97

Would you like to grow a large following on Linked-in? 101

Pinning your hopes on Pinterest? 109

Use Colour Psychology to Increase sales. 115

Use YouTube, visual media and visual storytelling to improve your brand 127

Meerkat and Periscope put you live in front of your Customers. 137

Snapchat advertising 144
Building your Instagram community 146
Short videos on Vine 154
The 8 part tool recipe for saving time on social media 156
The power is in the list 160
What is the future of Social Media? 166

Introduction.

This book is designed to give you a deeper insight into what Social Media is, its various formats and how to get the best out of it both for business and for fun too. I hope you enjoy it and learn some interesting hints and tricks to increase your Social presence along the way.

All over the World businesses are raising their social brand and increasing both customer numbers and sales all through the power of Social Media.

Also, people are making new friends and in some instances life partners. You too can benefit from this fast growing medium, if you haven't started to already!

Read on and I'll show you how to utilise the power of social media to both improve your business as well as your personal life.

You will learn the tricks, tips and hacks used by some of the main social media gurus to enable you to really establish yourself on social media. I have tried to cram it with as many ideas as possible to increase your online visibility.

What is Social Media?

Let's start by trying to define what Social Media is.

Almost all of you will have used the World Wide Web or just 'web' as it's also known. Initially it was designed as a communication tool to get messages sent between two or more different people. In actual fact, the messages are in a format called 'hypertext'.

The World Wide Web was invented by Sir Tim Berners-Lee back in 1989. He was a CERN Scientist and he had designed it as a method of communicating various formats of information in a much faster way than was then possible.

Together with another Scientist Robert Caillau they worked on a proposal to create the 'web' and the first incarnation of the Web was created in a rough format by Christmas 1990 with the first web browser and first web pages (written about the project itself) all created at the same time.

In August 1991 the World Wide Web was launched as a public service (many people consider August 23rd to be its launch date as this was when new users had access to it).

In 1993, CERN announced that the World Wide Web would be available to everyone for free. Following this a graphical browser was introduced for the World Wide Web by a team from the University of Illinois at Urbana-Champaign. This innovation meant that graphics could easily be added to text in messages, swiftly making the World Wide Web the World's favourite tool for communication.

Over time, Website Developers and Application (App) Designers started looking at ways to get more intricate uses from the World Wide Web. The term Web 2.0 was coined and referred to websites that allowed users to collaborate and interact in a virtual community.

Sir Tim Berners-Lee said his original vision was "a collaborative medium, a place where we all meet and read and write".

This brings us back to our original question...what is social media? In Web 2.0 terms it would be a website or App that allows two-way communication of ideas. This differs from regular media (like newspapers, magazines, books, TV and film etc.) where you are presented with the information with no instant method of reply.

Social Media allows the transfer of text, graphics, photos, audio and visual in a seamless, integrated manner. It has enabled people from all over the World to communicate thoughts and ideas instantly to each other.

Our use of the World Wide Web is growing more and more each year. The average number of minutes spent on the web was said to be accelerating at a tremendous speed doubling between 2011 and 2012

The number of registered social media users has increased from a million in 2004 to well over a billion in 2014.

In the United States people spend on average 16 minutes of every hour on Social Media sites and 47% of those people say that Facebook is their number one influencer for purchasing products with a quarter of users logging on at least 5 times daily *

Over 90% of Marketers use Social Media for business purposes with over 70% reporting it has gained them new business*

* source sociallystacked.com

10 reasons your business should be leveraging Social Media.

There are many, many reasons for your business to use Social media to increase sales and grow your customer base. Here is a list of my top ten reasons that your business needs to take action now.

1). By using social media in a consistent manner and putting out regular good quality content you WILL drive new business and increase the number of sales you are making. The majority of businesses have reported a gain in business particularly when using Facebook and Linked-in

2). Using social media gives you a completely free platform to put your content on. Obviously you have the option to buy advertising on all of the major social media platforms but this is not a necessity and therefore social media offers a cost-effective way for businesses on a tight budget to grow their online presence.

3). When you put content on social media you give your customers a chance to interact with you. This gives you a much more personal connection with them. It lets your customer see there is more to your company than just a 'sales machine'.

4) Through listening to your customer on social media, you can learn more about your customers likes, what they want, any comments about your brand and maybe even giving insights into potential future sales opportunities.

5). Social media is a great way to enhance your lead generation. It has been reported that over 70% of B2C companies generate leads through Facebook alone.

6). The more good, relevant content you post online on things like social networks, the more likes you will get back and therefore the search engines will start to see back links to your company website. This in turn will increase your position on the search engines when people are looking for you.

You should use your website to build trust and through its interactivity, foster relationships with people

7) Social Media allows you to grow your word of mouth sales. If people say good things or share your content with their customers, friends and family, it may build their trust in your products making it much more likely that they will buy from you.

8) Sometimes the content you post may grow viral. This means your content is getting shared by many people who are then sharing it with their friends and family. Ultimately this can lead to some posts being seen by millions of potential buyers which will create a long and lasting buzz about your products. When this happens there is a good chance to monetise your content by allowing links to adverts to be placed on it.

9) By posting regular content online in blogs, forums and other social media message boards; you can establish yourself as an expert with your existing and potential customers

10). It's a great way to explain the quality of your products, what you do and why customers should choose to buy from you

Main social media sites and which ones are the correct fit for your business?

The top social media sites in the Western World are: Google +, Facebook, Twitter, Instagram, Linked-in and Bebo. In general, users have to be thirteen years and older to hold accounts apart from Linked-in where users have to be 18 years plus to join (mainly as this site is aimed exclusively at business users).

Google+ claims to have 1.6 billion registered users whilst Facebook have 1.4 billion active users every month.

Twitter has about half the amount of users but is growing the quickest of all of the main Social Media sites with Instagram now rapidly closing too.

What Is the Importance of Conducting a Social Media Audit?

Before writing any content whatsoever, you will need to do a Social Media Audit to determine and locate all of your Social Media Profiles i.e. which accounts you have set up on all of the Social Media Networks (not only the likes of Facebook, You Tube, Google + etc. but also the content submitted on lesser known networks like Quora and Reddit. Many of the main social media platforms, such as Facebook and Twitter, also have their own suite of analytical tools to assist you in your aims.

Before starting your audit you need to think about what you are trying to achieve as a business through Social Media and ensure you measure against this (you can include things like calculating the return on Investment on your Social Media Campaigns and the rate your social media following is growing)

You should ensure your Audit includes determining the demographic of your customers on each Social Media Platform. The information you need includes:

- Sex of your customer

- Average age of your customer (even if it's banded 18-80 years)

- Location of your customer (you can use geo location with lots of the paid advertising platforms these days in order to target specific, local traffic).

- What are your customers interests both business and social?

You should also ask things like what are their problems that need solving?

Also, look to see that you're content across all of the Social Media platforms is consistently branded; each profile is completed correctly and also takes a look to see if there are any unofficial sites out there for your business made by past employees, or just fans of yours.

Other things to measure Include:

How good are the company at getting their message across and amplified by their customers?

What type of content is being produced and at what frequency?

What is the monthly and annual budget for Social Media split by platform?

What feedback you are receiving as a result of publishing your information (you could measure the number of retweets, likes etc.).

You need to ensure that your content is standardised across all platforms (meaning your corporate colours are used and/or your company logo or Typeface is consistently displayed. That the Information given is current and accurate and that your customers are receiving a quick response to their feedback.

The levels of customer service offered on Social Media will have a direct Impact on your levels of business

Put all of the information you find into a spreadsheet showing the web address and number of followers and how much content has been published to each site as well as the content creator if several people or different companies create your content.

It also may help to keep records of User names and passwords for each, at this stage. This may be invaluable to you later if someone leaves your business, or even misplaces the log-in details. It will also enable you to take swifter action in the event of a security breach.

Once you have completed your initial audit, take some time to look at the results on your spreadsheet to familiarise yourself with how you believe you are performing

Next, take a look at what your biggest rivals are doing on the Social Networks? You can use a tool to do this to save you time (Something like SEMrush will really help with this- it costs $69 per month for the paid version but there is a smaller, free version available.) Another great place to look is socialmention.com.

For now I want you to focus on your rival's overall performance on Social Media.

So having looked at your rival's performance on the Social Media networks, how do they compare to yours? Are they doing better? IS there anything you could do better? Any ideas you can replicate (I didn't say copy)?

You now have all of the information at your fingertips and can take a much more well-informed decision as to which networks you are doing well on, which you are doing badly on and which networks your rivals are focussing their efforts on.

Once, you have worked out your key demographics then it is much easier to write content that will appeal to your target audience.

Write quality content to expand your social networks.

Content is a way of getting your brand, thoughts and information to your target audience. This can be in the form of articles, blogs, info graphics, e books, webinars and the like.

Social Media Content is not meant to be a one way thing, once written, you have made your point to your readers and it is forgotten. It is meant to be a two-way conversation which hopefully will lead to other conversations

Social media sites can be further subdivided into categories; the following list is by no means a comprehensive one but instead focuses on some of the more popular networks.

Social networking sites: - Facebook, Linked-in, My Space and Bebo

Blogging sites such as WordPress and Blogger.

Micro blogging Sites: such as Tumblr and Twitter

Social encyclopaedia sites like: Wikipedia and Wikihow and the notorious WikiLeaks

Social virtual world gaming: second life, world of Warcraft, the Sims, and IMVU

There are social bookmarking sites such as Reddit, Digg and Stumble upon

Photo display: Instagram, Pinterest and Cinema gram.

Video sharing: YouTube and Vimeo

Of course there are thousands of other sites too numerous to list here. Many social media sites can now be classified in several of the different categories shown above. For instance, Facebook have recently launched their video auto play system and have through this become one of the World's largest video sharing sites.

1) Most of us are busy people leading ever increasingly high tempo lives where there just aren't enough hours in the day to do what we planned.

2) We are constantly being bombarded with information, whether that is from emails, videos, news, blogs, the telephone etc.

3) With the rise in smart phones and tablets we are able to connect to this information more or less whenever we choose. It's almost as if we interconnected with the Internet.

Because of these factors, most of us dip in and out of being on the Internet.

We wake up in the morning and we may go on Facebook to check our friends, family or colleagues status enquiries, or we may look at our phones to read the news or tweet an interesting article we've come across.

So what does that mean when we want to get our information out there to others? It means we are competing for our target's time. They have a massive choice now over how to divide their time up.

In order for your information to be read by others you will need to make it as good as you can to stand out from the crowd, so that your item is the one being read when somebody has five minutes before their next meeting or before the kids come home from School etc.

Take for example this headline:

How I trebled my Facebook followers in less than three days!

It sounds impressive doesn't it? But, in reality I could have just increased the number of Facebook followers I had from one to three followers. It's all about framing your content.

Therefore, to have a chance of your previous work being read, your headlines need to be kept short, sharp and interesting.

If possible you should include a relevant, interesting image to make your post really stand out.

Another thing you want to think on is how much time do you plan to spend each day on Social Media, both providing content and also interacting with your customers, friends and family?

Let's take a look at the various types of content you may want to consider producing.

A website

Remember, with any content you have just a few seconds to persuade your audience to stay.

This is the first thing you need to think about when creating content for social media. Think of it as your home, a place where customers can come to visit you, interact with you and buy your products (which I'm sure are of a splendidly high quality).

A good example of this is:

www.mumandbabyclub.com

Websites are ranked by the search engine owners by the quality and quantity of their content, as well as the number of visitors and other reputable sites linking to them.

Remember when creating your website it will take time for your site to rise up the search engine rankings. Google produce some excellent guides both written and in video for web masters to hone their craft.

Do not neglect your website or the need to be constantly introducing new and engaging content. If you can't think of anything to write, then get in some hired help. We shall discuss this later in more detail.

The latest websites are 'Responsive Design Websites' which mean they alter shape to fit whichever medium they are being viewed.

Today's media is viewed on mobiles, laptops, tablets, notebooks, wearables as well as PCs. It is imperative the precious content that you spent so long creating is able to be seen.

Once you have your website up and running, why not add a blog?

Tip- Submit your website to Reddit. You can get lots of extra traffic in this way. All you do is sign-up at Reddit.com and submit your website with a short description then choose a sub-Reddit (sub-category) to list it under

.

Remember- Don't forget to optimise your site for mobile users too. Most people these days access the Internet through either their phone, or tablet device. The number of people accessing the Internet through these devices is set to go up and up and you will miss a massive opportunity to get your brand to your target audience if your website is not optimised.

You should never consider your website to be completed. The more you add fresh content, the higher it will be ranked by the search engines and the more likely it will be for you to obtain new devotees of your site

Hint- Once you have finished your website and added some content to add an XML site map. This allows the search engine robots to find and rank your content more easily. If you have made your website using WordPress you will find several useful plugins to enable you to add a site map

You no longer have to submit your website to the search engines as they will find your site providing you write good quality content.

Blog

Short for weblog is a set of written thoughts, ideas or information written diary style and displayed as entries called ' posts'. Usually they are shown in reverse chronological order.

Nobody will read your blog if the quality of your content is of no use to them or doesn't entertain. Keep it Interesting and informative. Ask yourself.'What are my readers getting from this'? Is it helping them? Try to write it in a style that 'talks to them individually

When writing your blog, try to remember to keep it laden with keywords based on the title of your article. The search engines will focus on the first paragraph of your blog (usually between 100-120 words).

Remember to try to keep your blog natural sounding. After all it still needs to be read by your subscribers. A typical blog will be 8-900 words although they can vary wildly in length. Top blogs are now looking to write multiple articles of 2000+ words

Blogs can rank much faster in the major search engines than web pages. It is possible to be ranked for your blog within a couple of hours.

Try sending your blog to article marketing sites. If it is accepted you can get some useful back links which will increase your ranking.

Recently there has been a trend towards multi-author blog sites with guest writers. These compilation blog sites often make it to the top of the search engine rankings due to the amount of authors, content and all of their followers providing the necessary backlinks.

It has been proven that companies that blog have over 400% more indexed pages than those that don't.

Some of the best bloggers today have become 'overnight sensations' with their blogs making millions of pounds in the process

Infographics

You can really generate a lot of buzz about your product or industry with Infographics

An infographic is short for Information Graphic. As the name suggests an infographic is information and data produced with the aid of graphics to best depict the information.

For instance an infographic could show the percentages of adults who go to sleep before and after midnight and their age groups.

Tip-Personally, I like to use a fantastic App called Canva to create infographics, as well as other types of visual media.

Canva provides a number of templates for all sorts of design work, including templates for emails, blog graphics, Facebook and Twitter headers, Facebook posts and many others.

They also feature an On-line Design School for those less experienced in visual display, showing how to create different types of graphic colour and font combinations and other best practices for making your graphics look better.

If you can't or won't design infographics you can quite easily get them on a site like upwork.com or fiverr.com.

Memes

Memes are defined by Wikipedia as an idea, behaviour or style which spreads from person to person within a culture.

Great sites for checking out the most popular memes are:

Reddit and also:-

www.knowyourmeme.com

You can even add your own words to pre-designed graphics to create your own memes.

Tip-I would like to recommend a great iOS App called 'Over' where you can add text to any of your photos. There's a great choice of fonts and graphics to add style and make your own meme in no time at all.

Video

Video comes in all shapes and sizes from homemade videos to explainer videos for businesses.

If you're lucky your video will get so many views it will grow viral. When this happens, it gets shared so many times that it becomes an Internet phenomenon.

Video and audio combined is the best form of media to show your product or service. That is because the brain finds it easier to remember and understand things shown and spoken at the same time.

I find the use of animation to be a great way to increase my sales. I use both whiteboard animation (as the name suggests this is basically text written on a white board a Videoscribe.co offer a great subscription package for this which not only gives a choice of different pens, implements to write with and colours and textures of paper, but also a great selection of vector based graphics.

Another system to use to create great intros is Videomakerfx. This great video making system features a number of avatars who appear alongside words shown in different graphical formats.

According to www.cmo.com over 40% of US marketers report increased engagement rates when messages contain some form of video.

Almost three quarters of video ads are watched to their completion and customers are 27% more likely to click through to your product when a video is included.

They also report US spending on digital video will double from $4 billion in 2015 to $8 billion in 2016.

Creating content quickly

For Social Media purposes, you, or your team will need to create regular content. For SEO purposes and getting the most eyeballs on your work, it can often be the case of the longer and more topics (i.e. keyword) specific, the better.

There has been a trend of late to build articles of at least two thousand words long. It also would appear that Google give a higher ranking for longer articles.

So, what's the quickest way of getting content out there? Well, most people can speak much faster than they can type (that includes me.) Let's look at a way we can get content mostly from your spoken words

Therefore, the best way to quickly get your content out there is to start off by getting a piece of paper and noting down the title of your content and the different sub-headings, or points you want addressed in your content. You'll end up with a list of say a dozen, or so different sub-headings on your piece of paper. An average English word consists of 4-5 characters and most of us can type at approximately 50 words per minute, on average. Some professional typists can get to 90 words per minute. However, we can speak much faster than we can type, with many of us talking at 120-130 words per minute.

So, the next thing you need to do is grab either a Dictaphone, or, if you have a smartphone (most of us have these days), download a voice recorder App. You can than talk through the different points on the sheet, covering them in greater detail i.e. using your written sheet for prompts as to what to say whilst recording yourself speaking. Yes, it takes some getting used to, but, it's a great way of dumping the knowledge locked away in your head out into the open

Once you're happy with what you've recorded you'll find you have very quickly compiled a long piece of content. The next thing you will need to do is to get it transcribed down into writing. There are a number of transcription services available. You can hire someone on Fiverr.com to transcribe your audio. Alternatively, one of the mist recommended services is from a site called Rev.com who offers a really fast transcription service for just $1 per minute. Your finished product will be delivered to you within 24 hours.

Next, you will need to go through your transcribed product and just ensure everything is as it's meant to be

and then it's ready to publish. You'll find this method much quicker and cost-effective in the long run than your or a team member sitting and typing every article.

If you don't wish/can't afford to use a transcription service, there are also some transcription Apps you can download onto your phone, which will attempt to turn your words into writing as you speak.

One of the best of these Apps is Dragon Dictation software. I've used this myself and would say it's

Approximately 90% correct on transcribing my voice. So, if you don't mind spending a bit of time editing what you've had transcribed, then this will still save you time and money and more importantly make you or your Staff members, more productive in the long run

Content and SEO

We cannot really talk about written content without briefly talking about SEO (search engine optimisation)

This is one of the main methods (apart from advertising by you which you will gain people to come to look and hopefully read your content.

Without SEO you will be hard pressed to get people to come to view your content as it is one of the main ways that the search engines such as Google and Bing will place your content in their lists of most important sites, articles or videos when people are searching for content similar to yours.

On page SEO is not that difficult to do and when creating your content you should always have at the back of your mind thoughts on how you will add long-tail keywords into your content.

I have covered Niches and long tail keywords in my Udemy Course 'How to make passive Income from Affiliate Marketing for Beginners.'

Alternately, if you need to learn more about this subject there are a number of resources available online.

Remember, any SEO changes you make to your site will not bring an immediate improvement to your sites search engine rankings as these things take time to work through (usually weeks or months)

Nine tips for increasing your click through rates on your Facebook Ads.

When you are thinking of a social media network, Facebook is the largest of them all. Formed in 2004 and previously known as The Facebook its chairman is Mark Zuckerberg and it is now one of the most famous brands on the planet

As of January 2015 Facebook boasts almost 1.4billion Monthly users or, almost 900 million daily users. Its users watch 3 billion videos and give 7 billion likes. There are also 1 billion daily searches.

It also makes billions of dollars in revenue every year for this now publicly owned company. In 2013 alone it made over 7 billion dollars.

As Facebook is the biggest social media platform of the lot and therefore some of the biggest gains for your business can be had on Facebook?

Facebook users are fairly evenly split with slightly more females logging on daily (I know my Wife spends large amounts of time on it, following her Friends every movement. The highest traffic on the site occurs midweek between 1-3pm although the highest levels of engagement is on Thursday and Fridays.

Over 40% of Marketers claim Facebook is critical for the success of their business. Because of this it is very likely that your competitor is on Facebook actively trying to grow their brand. Therefore, it is important that you also cultivate your brand on this Social Media platform.

The top nine ways to increase click through rate on Facebook ads are:

1. Make the title interesting. It really needs to stand-out. Your customer has to be interested in your product.

2. Keep your title to eight words and under (preferably under 50 characters). Humans have a very short attention span (recently proven to be less than a goldfish).

3. Include pictures or videos in your subject matter. This will make your customers want to stay longer.

4. Asking a question in your title will also work.

5. Use A/B Split testing on different formats of ads to ensure which works best. Use Facebook power editor to enable you to do this

6. An article with both pictures and a list makes the item more interesting to readers.

7. Offer something of value for free such as a downloadable PDF or a free e book. The science of Reciprocity refers to responding to a positive action with another positive action and then rewarding kind actions. This means the customer is more likely to buy from you after receiving your kind gesture.

8. Odd number lists seem to work better than even number lists (hence the nine items on this list).

9. Best Images to use are of a woman smiling, a child or a pet. They appeal to a wider audience

The Ninja way of attracting customers on Facebook

You may not have heard of them but Dark Posts really are the best way to target traffic on Facebook without any of your competitors seeing what you're doing.

The main difference between Dark Posts and Usual Posts is that they won't appear on your Facebook wall and so in effect, are invisible to everyone apart from your target.

The second difference is you can target by Keywords (for example Company Owner etc.).

To make a Dark Post open up the Power Editor and select Manage Pages from the drop-down selection menu.

Next, choose the page for which you're making the post. Then, in the main area click 'create post button.' Then you'll see the create Unpublished Page Post.

Choose the type of post type from the selection along the top (Link, Photo, Video, Status or Offer), and then complete the information for your post.

Ensure you select This Post Will Only Be Used as an Ad (bottom left) so it won't appear on your Facebook page.

Next, choose keywords for the interests which meet your selection criteria. Then select Create Post.

The post will be saved to your list of posts. When you're ready to publish your post, select it from the list and select 'Create Post.'

With dark posts you can target specific people but you aren't crowding your wall as the posts remain invisible. Hence, that is why these posts are called "dark."

The Five whys and how they're Important for your Social Media strategy

In Social Media it's our aim to get our message to as many people as possible and for those people to both like and engage in us and our content and then pass on our message to their friends, family and other followers (In other words to make them go viral.)

So, how does a business ensure the content they are delivering is based on their core business?

Developed by Sakichi Toyoda, Founder of Toyota Industries, the 'five whys' is a system of answering questions to understand what the core purpose of each business is and therefore it makes promoting your brand that much easier.

So let's take a closer look at the five whys. At its heart it's designed to look past a problem to the deeper underlying cause and then to keep asking questions until the cause is eliminated. In every occasion you should ask no fewer than five questions.

This can be used for solving problems in all areas including Social Media.

Take this problem as an example

Our fictional company ' Trevor's Wholesalers' had been unable to grow their Social Media reach and was losing business to their rivals.

They could ask the following series of questions (or whys):

Why isn't our message resonating with our followers? It is.

Why are our Competitors doing better than us?

We're not sure.

Why aren't we getting value for money on our Social Media Spend?

We aren't spending anything on advertising.

Why haven't we received a completed Social Media Audit?

We did, but haven't actioned it.

Why are we just relying on free advertising to increase our Social Media reach?

We were trying to save the Company money

Why were half of our Social Media team allowed to leave and not replaced?

We haven't had time to look for replacements.

In the end, the series of 'whys' provided an answer to the underlying cause. In this particular Company there was a massive underfunding on their Social Media Department. Management had received a Social Media Audit but filed it away. Key team members were lost and not replaced and their rivals had been allowed to get ahead.

The five whys method can be used in various areas of your business and life and is a useful method to add to your arsenal.

Reach your target audience on Twitter.

Twitter was launched on 15th July 2006. It is a micro blogging site where its followers put up 140 character micro blogs known as Tweets

Twitter has an audience of almost 300 million monthly active users. Those users tweet approximately 500 million tweets (or posts) a day. Most of them access their accounts from their mobile phones and three-quarters of the users are outside the US.

Twitter is another company making lots of money. In 2013 it made over 650 million dollars in revenue, although its market value has fallen of late.

It has recently been announced that tweets will once again show up in Google search following a deal between the two parties. Obviously this has massive implications for Ad revenues and it will now be increasingly important for businesses to have fresh content on Twitter.

Ever wondered how many fake followers are on your Twitter followers you have?

It is reckoned by some that many of the people that have most followers on Twitter have millions of fake accounts following them. It is normal for top celebs to have between 5-10% fake followers according to research conducted by www.statuspeople.com

When I'm building my Twitter Audience, I'm very careful to not follow just anyone who follows me. Before adding anyone I look at their profiles and the quality and number of tweets they have previously made.

Personally, I don't want to be offered 10000 fake followers for $5.

I prefer my audience to be real, live people who share interests with me. From a sales and brand building perspective, It Is far better to have 100 followers from the same niche i.e. SEO/Social Media in my case than 1000fake followers as it is far more likely they will Interact.

Obviously a few fake followers may 'slip through the net' but, by and large, I try to Police my Twitter account as best as possible. In fact, I've just checked my list and found two fake followers out of the thousands that follow me. Needless to say they have now been removed and blocked from my followers' list. Why not check your list now?

Tip: you can do that at fakers.statuspeople.com

From a personal, learning perspective my followers often tweet articles or information about the latest innovations happening in my field.

Nobody ever knows everything, including the so called 'experts' or 'gurus.' I will never grow too complacent to learn and it is very easy to become out of touch with your audience if you don't keep abreast of the latest developments in your particular niche.

Before posting anything on Twitter (you only get a maximum of 140 characters to write your message, status or comment) it is worth taking a few moments to think about what you are going to post.

When posting your content, it may be a good idea to shorten any links to other people's content by using a link www.bitly.com is ideal for creating this type of link. All you do is to copy and paste the link from the article you wish to post onto the relevant field on bitly and click on the 'Shorten' button.

It will then generate a much shorter link to the post.

This has the dual benefits of making your post look tidier as well as it is likely you will get more hits on your tweet.

Don't be scared of asking your followers to re-tweet any of your content. Asking for a re-tweet will result in you getting your post a several times higher number of retweets. Studies have shown sometimes the number of retweets can be over 20% higher

Top-Tweets with images linked to them will always get more attention. In order, to get the highest number of tweets you will need:

1) An attention grabbing headline

2) A great image

3) Great content

4) A shortened link

Tip- do you know you can check on exactly how well each tweet has done in connecting with your audience?

If you select on any tweet you have made half way down the page you will see a field entitled ' view tweet activity'. If you select on that you will get the number of impressions or views it has had together with the number of engagements (actions) made on the tweet such as re-tweeting, favouring, when someone has checked out your profile etc.

This can be a very useful tool when deciding what tweets you should concentrate on to engage your audience.

#Hashtags

A hashtag is simply a way of categorising your content into a specific subject or subjects to make them more easily found on search engines. The hashtag is placed before the word you wish to be ranked for. Make your hashtags relevant to the subject you are posting on.

Then once someone searches for either #social media or #SEO they will be brought to a list of sites containing the specific hashtag.

Hashtags can be used when posting content on all of the main Social Media networks such as Facebook, Twitter, you tube, Instagram, google+, Pinterest, Tumblr etc.

It is important not to make long lists of hashtags for any post. Otherwise your post will resemble a list of hashtags.

It is also important not to overuse hashtags and litter the same hashtags over and over again throughout the body of your blog, or other content. This is known as hashtag spam.

The hashtags with the highest number of searches for them (based on area and social connections) will then be known to be 'trending'. This is useful to remember as you can search for the hashtags trending on Twitter or other social networks nationally, or, in your local area.

For example I have just typed in to Google the following search ' trending in the U.S.' and had a string of subjects come up with the top one #blizzardof2015. Now if I sold something like warm weather clothes, or ski boots etc. and wanted to join in that conversation I would just then search for the hashtag and be presented with a whole heap of places to comment and potentially grow my brand and sales.

You can also create your own hashtag to promote your brand but if you do this make sure it is very specific and unlikely to be misread or mistaken for something or someone else. In the past, .many mistakes have been made by people or companies using hashtags.

If your hashtag is strong enough and your readers start to use it then every time they see the hashtag they will be reminded of you.

So if I were writing content based on social media and SEO, I could use the hashtags #social media #SEO.

Once you have posted your content on Twitter it can help to use a call to action in your Tweets. Things like Subscribe now, Download, Get your free gift, free eBook, free whitepaper; all encourage more hits on each of your tweets.

If you are looking for more people to view your content, don't be afraid of re-using it by just changing the title slightly.

Do you know you can register your hashtag at www.whatthetrend.com Go there and give your hashtag a description and get it registered before anyone else does.

Best Apps for use with Twitter.

There are a growing number of Apps designed to make your Tweeting easier, more efficient and to enable you to grow your followers at an accelerated rate

Apps like Tweet deck really enhance the functionality of Twitter.
Use it to personalise your timeline so visitors get to see your tweets in the preferred order of your choice.

Unfollow- get to see in an instant the people who have stopped following you, the people you follow but who don't follow you back and also, those who have followed you but you haven't followed back. It also has useful features like a display of those who haven't tweeted for long periods of time.

Twitter Advanced Search Facility

Another great feature in Twitter is the advanced search facility where you can find out what people are saying about you or your competitors.

If you want to explore tweets sent from London in the first week of February that mention Katy Perry it can do that too!

For instance, I have just written a book entitled 'Help! I'm scared of Spiders'.

By inputting the phrase 'I'm scared of Spiders' into the advanced search engine I get a list of Twitter users who have mentioned they are scared of Spiders. It is then easy for me to reply to their tweets informing them of my great book which will help them with their fears and at the same time increase my sales figures.

You could easily use the search engine to look for phrases relating to the business you are in, such as 'looking for a logo' or 'need to find a plumber' etc. You can also combine that with the search for the local area i.e. 'looking for a logo' as well as searching for the area 'London'.

Growing circles on Google+

I absolutely adore Google+ and I'm not the only one as Google claim that over 540 million use their Google+ product every month.

Because of this it is worth adding all of the people from your Gmail Contact list into your Google+ Circles. Think of circles as groups of people split into Family, Friends, Acquaintances, Colleagues and Customers. You include anyone into more than one circle.

When posting on google+ try to keep your headlines to ten words or less.

Any social media post should have a great headline to increase engagement. Also ensure you use images to enhance your posts.

Because Google+ is run by Google you can be pretty sure that any decent content put on there will appear high up the Google search rankings.

Were you aware that you can have a video conference call for up to 10 people on Google+ using hangouts?

Google+ Hangouts on Air are a great YouTube addition, where you can show videos with a minute-by-minute directory on top. Right now, it seems Google+ fans are the ones taking regular advantage of it, and I'm unsure why when it's so great. Perhaps, people either haven't heard of it? It can deliver long videos all in one shot. The post is then given its own URL and viewers can bookmark it for reference.

One of the most important features of Google+ is its Business Listing function. Google My Business help increase the visibility of your business on both local and mobile search

Would you like to grow a large following on Linked-in?

Linked-in has over 330 million users. About half of these are active monthly users. It adds 2 new members per second to its business-orientated social networking site. I use it regularly to grow my network of business contacts and would suggest you do the same.

I built my Linked-in account from zero to over 6000 real followers in just a few weeks. All of the people I've added are decision makers for their companies like Company Owners, CEO's, Presidents, or Vice Presidents, Directors or other senior board members or executives. In other words, they can be classed as highly targeted sales leads.

The first and most important thing to do on Linked-in is to ensure your profile page is as complete as you can make it.

This is the equivalent to your personal sales page. It showcases you and as such you should spend the relevant amount of time ensuring that as much detail is included as possible

Remember to fill in as much information as possible. As you improve your profile Linked-in will assign you a rating. The aim is to get the All-star rating which is the top award for completion of your profile.

The easiest way to increase the number of your Linked-in followers is to simply follow the people who follow your followers, In that way, your followers should remain broadly in the same niche as you are in. (I know that last paragraph may take some re-reading).

Linked-in allow you to follow 200 people more than follow you. On top of this, people who know you and are in the same industry will soon be following you as they want follow-backs.

(As an aside, I usually turn down requests from recruitment agencies as I don't want my followers or myself to be hounded by recruiters or the like without first getting their permission. Obviously, if you're job hunting, please ignore this paragraph.)

Once you have made the initial connection the aim is to turn that connection into a 'real' customer.

One of the best ways to engage your customers is to like and comment on posts they make. You'll often see announcements that X has been in a job for Y amount of years, or they may have gotten a new Job. It takes hardly anytime at all to congratulate them. It is also worthwhile sharing your prospects posts.

The trick is to get a nice balance between sharing, commenting and liking whilst at the same time not coming across as some crazed stalker, because this will mean you get absolutely no chance of a sale.

The aim is to slowly increase the level of interaction over time between you and your prospect.

This way long term friendships are made, making for a potential customer that is more likely to stay with you for a prolonged period of time.

Linked-in has some great ways to search for comments posted by your followers.

You can search by either the top comments or most recent posts made by your contact.

Once you have completed your profile to your satisfaction (and I mean completed all of it not just parts) start to join some 'groups'. Concentrate only on the groups that fall into your niche.

Once you have joined a group you will see the list of group members. Some groups have millions of members. You can then 'cherry pick' those you would like to link to. More often than not they will link back to you and your network will grow exponentially.

I often have dozens of requests from people wishing to link-in with me. It is fairly easy to grow a vast network. Linked-in allow you to join up to 50 groups and therefore, you could be promoting to a much wider audience than you do currently.

However, once you have made the initial connection the aim is to turn that connection into a 'real' customer.

Another important thing to remember is after you have created your personal page to check whether your company has a page too. If it doesn't, then you need to create one. This doubles your chances of making new connections.

Pinning your hopes on Pinterest?

In my opinion Pinterest is the dark horse in the Social Media race

Pinterest was formed in 2010. It is a social network which offers its subscribers the chance to create a 'virtual scrapbook' of their favourite websites, items, Pages etc. which are displayed on 'boards'. These boards are usually arranged by theme. Boards can then be viewed or shared by other subscribers.

It has approximately 70 million subscribers. 80%+ of Pinterest users are women although that's not to say there isn't plenty of things for men to like about Pinterest too.

Users can grab content from other Pinterest boards and show them on theirs. They can also take content from outside of Pinterest by using the 'pins it' button. It's a simple system and it works

According to some statistics by Main Street Host, Pinterest accounts for more than 90% of Social shares. Just imagine the power of posting your products on Pinterest!

That's why you'll find most of the World's leading brands on there. This is a Social Media site you cannot afford to underestimate or ignore.

Pinterest drives more traffic to ecommerce sites than all of the top methods put together.

Its customers spend more money than on any other platform.

So, how do you get your share of the pie from Pinterest and find the perfect thing to pin?

Firstly, try to pin original pins on Pinterest.

That will put you head and shoulders above lots of other people on there as over 80% of traffic on Pinterest is re-pinned traffic

According to www. expandedramblings.com. Pins without faces are re-pinned 20% more than those with faces and pins that are lighter tend to be preferred over darker coloured pins.

You also need to build more followers in the same way as you do on any other Social Media Sites. If you follow people or re-pin their pins then a percentage of them will follow you back.

Don't forget to add the Pinterest follow button to your website or blog and pin your website content regularly

Tip- comment on popular pins. You want to show people you know and are concerned or care about the subject. This will attract more interest to you and your pins.

Mention others in your pins and consider complimenting them on their product, pin or blog. This will heighten their awareness of you.

Run a competition on Pinterest offering a prize. For instance, I make courses for Udemy. I could offer access to my top-selling course ' How to get amazing Income from Fiverr! Fiverr Hacks and Tips' for free to the first five to follow you and pin their favourite make money working from home tip on your board.

Finally, keep your followers happy by pinning relevant content on a regular basis. This is all about providing value for them. If you build your followers you will be able to reap the rewards.

Use Colour Psychology to Increase sales.

There are a number of ways you can use psychology to increase your social media likes and sales. Everything from the font a post is written in to the colour of your web page can send signals to your readers about your brand on things like class, trust-worthiness and several other qualities which will distinguish you from your competition

For instance, kiss metrics have produced the following statistics based on the colours used in websites:-

Women don't like Grey, orange, and brown. They like in order, blue, purple, and green.

Men don't like purple, orange, and brown. Men like blue, green, and black.

Let's take a look at the colours mentioned above what they signify. We'll take a look at the disliked colours first:

Grey- when talking about Grey we think of a boring, drab tone. It's a neutral colour which can look dull and even dirty. It is very conservative and emotionless.

It's also associated with older people as our hair turns grey as we get into the middle year as of our lives and so also signifies that middle-life wisdom, intelligence and security.

It's the colour of camouflage used by many Navies and Air forces.

If you are going to use grey on a website to signify intellect or security try to balance it with another colour.

On a colour wheel most other colours will combine particularly yellow/orange and blue/green tones. You may also blend it with pink and purples to give your site a more feminine quality.

Orange- we associate orange with flowers and the fun and happiness of spring and summer which comes after long, cold winters.

Orange is also bright and bold and combines the happiness that yellow signifies together with the energy of red. It signifies energy and healthiness and you'll often see vitamin tablet boxes and products aimed at children in this colour.

However, it is a colour that many people also dislike as it signifies a flamboyance and success that many people find annoying. Many Sports teams use this colour to show their fun but energetic sides.

It is used in many places to show construction areas and also for traffic cones and is therefore a sign of action.

If you're going to put a call to action button on your website use a big orange button (known in the industry as BOB).

Brown- what do we think of with the colour brown (apart from the obvious colour of sewerage), we think of leaves going brown, the arrival of colder, shorter, less happy days. It also is the colour of the earth, trees and some types of stone, showing a warm neutral colour with a certain dependency and naturalness associated with it. The American firm UPS uses it to good effect in their corporate branding.

If you are going to use it on a website, match it with other natural colours like green, yellow or orange.

Purple- this is the most contentious of the disliked colours as it's disliked by men but liked by women. Most people think that women prefer pink but if you look at the aforementioned lists. It'd be purple rather than pink women prefer.

Purple was used by the Ancients Romans to show power and wealth. It is often associated with royalty or nobility and is a mixture of the calmness and stability of blue together with the energy of red.

Using the colour purple shows you are sensitive, compassionate and understanding. It can be used by luxury brands to show wealth, wisdom, dignity together with all of the other traits we would associate with a king or queen.

So why don't men like purple? Maybe, it's an inherited, deep-seated hatred of royalty going back to the days when ancient battles were fought for and against King and Country. Or maybe, men do not like to be in touch with the caring, compassionate side that purple represents?

Now let's take a look at the favourite colours for websites:-

Blue- most people like the colour blue. It's the colour of both the sky and of the sea and symbolises safeness, trust, calmness, truth, responsibility, conservatism and loyalty. It can also be used to show both spirituality and heaven.

Blue promotes relaxation and reduces stress.

We often use Blue for a baby boy.

Most Social Media networks use the colour blue. Think of the logos of both Facebook and Twitter. Blue can be combined with white or the warm colours like red, orange and yellow.

Avoid using it with Food websites as blue is the colour of dieting.

Green- reminds us of nature and is the colour of grass, trees and bushes.

It signifies the growth of plants and flowers in spring and summer, the harmony and growth of nature together with safety, the green of traffic lights and progress.

We expect to see green when we think of outdoor events and of charities and environmental causes.

It's also the colour of money and signifies prosperity and abundance and therefore had an association with financial services and markets.

It mixes well with yellows and Browns.

Black shows elegance, luxury, power and sophistication. It also makes us think of night and the air of mystery of the unknown. Black absorbs light and the colour is used as protection both from the sun and also worn in mourning. Black shows control and power. It is also a very sophisticated tone.

When we think of black, we think of that little black dress or a tuxedo we wear to high-powered social events or that shining black sports cars.

You will find black (mixed with white for contrast) on a lot of luxury item websites. It shows items of great value. It should be noted that too much black signifies depression and coldness so use it sparingly.

The highest-converting colours for calls to action are bright primary and secondary colours such as red, orange, yellow and green.

Darker colours have very low conversion rates, so try to avoid them if you can.

Other colours to consider when designing content:-

White- is used to convey space and light. It is the colour of purity

Yellow- is used in warning signs such as traffic lights, hazards etc.

Red- is associated with blood and fire. It signifies power, passion and strength

Use YouTube, visual media and visual storytelling to improve your brand.

Many people don't realise that You Tube is the second biggest search engine in the World (behind Google). Billions of people regularly visit You Tube giving you an instant market to sell in. In fact, You Tube now has a billion active monthly users.

The people that post regularly on YouTube are known as Vloggers (short for video blogger) .Many have hundreds of thousands of followers who trust their opinion on products and value their advice. Products have been known to sell out in hours when they are mentioned by a Vlogger.

One of the best known Vloggers at the moment is called Zoella. She has over 6 million subscribers to her various social media channels 12 million views on you tube and Vlogs about fashion and is in partnership with an online fashion store called Boohoo.

She recently had a book ghost written for her 'girl on-line 'which went straight to the top of the best-sellers lists. She sold 80,000 copies in a single week.

When making a video for YouTube it's important to grab your viewers' attention in the first ten seconds, otherwise they are unlikely to continue to be engrossed in your content.

Next, your main content followed by a fantastic Outro and most importantly a call to action such as a buy it now button or your web address.

There are many apps that allow you to make useable content for YouTube. Many people have recorded themselves on their mobile phones and just uploaded it straight to YouTube and have had hundreds of thousands of views but to add things like titles, graphics etc. you will need to use Apps.

The first one that any beginner turns to is Windows Live Movie Maker. Use this product to upload your film and then add titles, captions, music, and audio or splice together different videos. It also includes several animations and transition slides. I would say this is the ideal place to first get to grips with making a video.

If you're willing to spend some money, all of the videos I put together for my online courses are made on Camtasia. This has a large number of great features which make movie making so much easier including the ability to do screen capture and synchronise audio to whatever it is you're filming. There are also a large array of graphic headers and a selection of transition animations which make this a great tool to have at your disposal.

Another great App is the iMovie app for Apple users.

When posting on YouTube, In order to determine how successful each video has been it is not good enough to just view the number of people that have viewed each video. This is because visitors can click on your video, view 2 seconds of it and then click off again if they don't like it.

YouTube offer a great free tool called 'YouTube Analytics' which will help you optimise your channel. It has in common with other analytics sites a way to learn about the demographics of your visitors, as well as informing you of where they are coming from.

It also has an excellent way of viewing the metrics and can give feedback on estimated minutes watched, monitored playbacks, total earnings, subscriber numbers and a whole host of other things.

Using their multiple line graph format you can view the performance of up to 25 videos and compare them like-for-like. These can be viewed as stacked graphs too. For those who like to play with graphs you get to look at your data in a whole host of other formats too including pie and bar charts.

Also, there is an interactive world map showing where in the world your videos are being played. If you move your mouse over each country you will get to see the individual statistics for each country.

Anyone can start a YouTube Channel. In fact, many people are making a fortune by making videos of them doing everyday things. One woman recently gave up her full time job ad she was making more from appearing on YouTube with her pet Gerbils for two hours per week than she was from a full time job!

Only yesterday I read of an eight year old who reportedly earns $127,000 per month just for posting videos of her and her younger Sister making sweets on YouTube.* source Outrigger Media

To work out how much money you can make on YouTube, here is a basic equation to follow;

For every 1000 views you will earn approximately $2 of income. Now, this is a very rough approximation as the 'stars' of YouTube allegedly can make a lot more per click than that.

People love to watch people. It's an in-built fascination for many of us. Why not try to ride the gravy train by putting yourself out there on video too?

So, in order to get your videos noticed on You Tube, one of the most important things to concentrate on apart from your video is the thumbnail picture that is generated once your video has been uploaded. If you go into your YouTube account you will notice a small button which says 'customise thumbnail.'

I would advise you to then select a screenshot of your video which best represents the subject, then go over to canva.com and add some large, striking text to the graphic which explains what's happening.

It may also be worth setting your screenshot on a bright coloured background. The trend at present is to put the thumbnails on multi-coloured, stripes backgrounds but anything that makes your thumbnail stand out from the rest will do. Use large bold, text lettering.

If you're unsure of what I mean go over to YouTube and take and to see the thumbnails that stand out most to you when looking down a list of videos.

Meerkat and Periscope put you live in front of your Customers.

Meerkat.

With the latest Social Media sites you can 'live stream' your latest offering, news announcement, event etc, direct to your customers.

Meerkat was debuted at the SSW Conference in 2015. You can live message your customers and also schedule your streams in advance and tweet your customers about that

Once you start using it, all of your Twitter followers will receive a tweet about your Meerkat activity. So, they'll be notified of every tweet, comment, like and re-tweet (obviously there are disadvantages to this too).

If your followers download the app, they can comment, like, and then re-tweet any stream to their followers.

The downside to this is, everything you do on Twitter is relayed, which can become very annoying to them, particularly if you're very active on the Meerkat service.

Periscope.

Periscope is a live streaming App and has been around since spring of 2015 and is already claiming 10 million users, which is a very impressive growth rate by anyone's standard.

It is now solely owned by Twitter. This gives them a massive advantage over their major rivals Meerkat as the two vie for market share. However, this could all change in the coming months as Meerkat build its relationship with Facebook. Recently, Facebook themselves entered the live streaming world although this foray was restricted access for Celebrities only to use.

There's over 40 years' worth of video (in minutes) watched on Periscope every single day and they have two million daily regular users.

So, should you be venturing into the World of live-streaming? Well it very much depends on the Industry you're involved in. Personally, I can see massive advantages of using it in the Worlds of Online Marketing, Education and many more

It takes time to get used to it, but it could bring massive bonuses to both your business and your Sales

Blab

As I was getting towards the end of writing this book, yet another live video platform called 'Blab' has grown in popularity and then just as quickly closed down again. Such is the swiftness of change in the Social Media World, I'm sure it won't be the last.

The power of Chat Apps

Best Messaging Apps

*The traditional SMS text message is quickly becoming 'old hat', particularly in light of the launch of a number of easy-to-use messaging apps such as WhatsApp, Kik, Line and other apps which all offer free text messaging. And that's not even mentioning the options for sending emoticons or stickers, voice, video and file-sharing to other users.

Check out 9 of my favourite mobile chat apps:-

1. WhatsApp - currently the World's largest chat app
2. Line- used a lot by 'Gamers' for team chats
3. Kik- used by over 40% of American youth

4. Wickr- each message 'self-destructs' which are deleted at a pre-set time.

5. BBM (blackberry messenger) recently got a new lease of life after new apps came out.

6. Google Hangouts are great for small groups of up to ten people.

7. Facebook messenger- chat app for the World's largest social media platform

8. Snapchat - seen as the teenage picture sending app of choice

9. Skype - great for video conferencing with business partners.

Snapchat advertising

Snapchat has roughly 100 million monthly users. Approximately 70% of those users are women. About the same percentage are 25 years old and under.

This should be remembered when targeting your advertising for Snapchat and makes it ideal for certain types of product placement although I won't stereotype anyone here by suggesting anything in particular.

Snapchat has been the target of a massive bid from Facebook but has so far kept its independence and had recently announced a new advertising initiative called Discover.

This allows larger companies to have their own channels and effectively sub-let space on those channels to those wishing to advertise in that space

This is a clever move by Snapchat passing on the responsibility of finding advertising buyers to their media channel owners. It remains to be seen how variances in Costs per channel will pan out but it is definitely worth

The price being bandied about for advertising on Snapchat is an astonishing $750,000 per day (according to Ad week) but whether they do manage to continue to drive sales at that price remains to be seen.

Building your Instagram community

Instagram is an online social network designed to let you tell your story in pictures or video. It currently has over 300 million active users each month and is now owned by Facebook.

Statistics show that most Instagram users are in the 18-35 year age bracket.

Although Instagram is a purely visual based network, it is a very powerful way of getting your message across to your target audience.

The starting point for using any social media account is to come up with a great username. For business purposes, try to be consistent with this across all the different social media sites if possible. This allows your followers to quickly find you whether you're on Instagram, Facebook, Twitter, or any of the other sites. In the likely event that you're name has already been taken choose a name similar to your chosen one

When completing your bio let your readers know what your unique selling points are (USP) and what your followers will get from following you. I.e. news and tips about your new product, recipes, coupons etc.

Like most other forms of social media it is important not to post too often. For Instagram I'd suggest no more than 5-10 pictures a day maximum. If you post too often your audience may become less engaged.

Remember to use hashtags in your personal bio and under your posts to lead your target audience to your page. Try not to use more than six hashtags per post. It is also worthwhile researching the current top tags and seeing if they would be appropriate to use against any of your posts i.e. hump day etc.

Some people put hashtags of film or pop stars and sports clubs just to draw people to their posts even if the post has nothing to do with the person or product being hash-tagged, but, try to ensure any images you use are free for Commercial use.

Start to like other people's photos. You can to this by going to the home page and liking the most popular photos.

Also, check out your friends photos and ensure you have liked those too. If you have employees or colleagues encourage them to do the same.

Next, do a search on your niche (remember to use a hashtag before typing in the subject you're interested in e.g. #football) then simply like all of those that match your niche. You can also comment under others photos to create a higher level of interaction.

Once you start to gain followers, Why not run a competition and feature your customers using your products then display them on your page?

Instagram gives you the chance to put high quality, visual content online for all of your fans and potential customers. For greater impact, try not to put on more than one or two photos each day and remember to use different filters on your photos to make them stand out from 'the crowd'.

Ensure when you put your photos on that you are adding comments and posing questions to get interaction.

Having spent time on Instagram it would seem that users are very fond of selfies and it does add that personal 'face' to your business.

Hint- Link your Facebook, Twitter and other social media accounts with your Instagram account and you will find that followers will 'jump' from one medium to the other and like your posts and possibly comment on all platforms.

When posting photos don't forget to tag people to draw their interest in your posts and only post photos that you think other people will find interesting. People will not follow you if they think you're boring. Post regularly with good quality images.

Short videos on Vine

Vine is a social media site which allows it's users to share short videos which can be joined together. Looped or stop motion added. Vine allows a 6 second maximum for any video posted which means anyone posting have to get their message or idea across very quickly indeed.

Vine was started in June 2012 and bought by Twitter in October of the same year and boasts 140 million monthly active followers. It's a great place to provide short videos on the services or products you offer.

Vine shows a very random mix of videos, (some have been serious news events and even pornographic in their nature).although the top videos (vines) tend to be humorous.

Some of the top accounts have millions of followers all waiting to get their next '6 second fix' from their favourite vine hero.

All of the top ten accounts have more than 5 million followers

If you have a Twitter or Facebook Account, vines can show as an integrated video on your Feed.

Vine videos have code you can use to embed onto your web pages, if so desired.

Use the search bar to find niches or people to follow. Use the explore tab to find the most popular vines.

Vine also lists trending hash tags.

Cinema gram is another site very similar to vine but less popular.

The 8 part tool recipe for saving time on social media

When it comes to productivity with your social media marketing there are a number of products to help you. I categorise these as my ACE'S

1. Automate
2. Communicate
3. Engage
4. Schedule

When I look for time-saving tools, it's easy to grab ones that help in one or more of these areas.

Please find below some of the Apps I think will help you most in unlocking more spare time for you. After all, as the old adage goes time is money.'

Automate

Twibble- Add an RSS feed set your schedule and then shares your feed with others and Increase your audience.

Communication

Topsy- allows you to search and analyse the social web.

Hootsuite-connects you to over 35 popular social networks

Engagement

Gum road -sell your work directly to your audience whether it is music, films, books or courses.

Schedule

Buffer- makes it super easy to share any content you're reading.

Klout- schedule posts and measure your social reach with this great tool.

Commun.it - easy twitter management

The power is in the list

You may have heard of the phrase 'the power is in the list'? Have you noticed how often you are offered a free download, a free e book, or something else when you provide your email address to a Marketer?

The reason people are making you these offers is because they are desperately after your email address. It has been said that each email address has an individual value which varies according to the value of product being sold.

When you're online marketer builds a list of email addresses, each list they possess is worth 'x' amount of money in sales to them for every new product they launch. By sending you 'useful' regular emails and then finally details of the current product they are promoting, they know that they will get a percentage of people buy their product (value 'y').

The value of each sales campaign is fairly easy to work out the value of each email or subscriber to your site.

This is calculated as Value Y (value of sales) divided by Value X (number of email addresses/subscribers that buy your product)

Therefore, say you email the people on your customer list with your latest product and one hundred people purchase the product which costs $50 = $5000 (it works in any currency) divide this amount by the number of email addresses on your list (in this case we will say we have 1000 email addresses= Value X)

This gives us the total value of $5 per customer email address. From this you will know that every customer you get will be worth approximately $5 for each email address you acquire.

This is particularly useful when using pay per click or buying advertising from any source, as it will make you much more confident of purchasing advertising slots when you are sure you will get a positive return for your investment.

To capture emails to use for your business purposes you will need what is known as a sales funnel. This consists of four parts

1. A landing page on your website where visitors can enter their email address and any other details you may want to glean from them.

2. You will need an email reply service, something like a Weber or mail chimps are good quality examples.

An email reply service will enable you to collect the email addresses from your website and respond to those who reply.

Hack- Do you realise you can use an unused email address as a basic auto responder.

Go to the tool bar at the top and find where you're out of office or vacation mode is.

Put into out of office or holiday mode and construct a message thanking your customer for contacting you and either telling them you will get back to them or directing the user to your website, or affiliate link.

3. Something of value such as a free eBook or white paper to give to those customers who subscribe. It has been proven when you give someone a free gift then they are much more likely to buy your goods.

4. A method of selling your goods online. Most web hosting sites offer an all in one online shop facility allowing you to take payments from PayPal and the like

What is the future of Social Media?

As technology has progressed we are now able to access Social Media on far more than the original PC's it was designed for. In today's World Social Media can also be communicated on our mobile phones and tablets, on watches and on things like Google Glass. The future of wearable technology is becoming brighter as our quest for even more ways to allow us to interact with each other.

Also, as time goes by, more data is being collected on all of us. Our likes and dislikes and even our habits are being collected and compiled.

Predictive Marketing is the future. You will hear more and more references to Big Data as time goes by. Marketing is becoming so refined that companies like Facebook probably know you better than you know yourself. It is the ultimate aim of Marketers to offer you goods before you even realise you want or need them

Big data can be used by all types of Companies, Marketers and Authorities. Police are already using it in places to predict where and when the next crime is likely to happen

In China, Sina Weibo is used as their preferred choice of Social Media Platform. In fact, it's not so much as a social media platform, but has managed to integrate with their whole way of life. For instance, when they go into some Restaurants they connect up to look at the menu on the same platform, order their food on Weibo, pay on Weibo and then leave a review on Weibo.

As you can see things are much more integrated there. Is this the shape of things to come for us all here? Only time will tell

www.ingramcontent.com/pod-product-compliance
Lightning Source LLC
Chambersburg PA
CBHW070300190526
45169CB00001B/485